LIGHT

Isaac Asimov

photography by Allen Carr

Follett Publishing Company Chicago

ISBN 0695-85165-9   Trade Edition
ISBN 0695-45165-0   Titan Edition
Library of Congress Catalog Card Number 70-85948
First Printing I

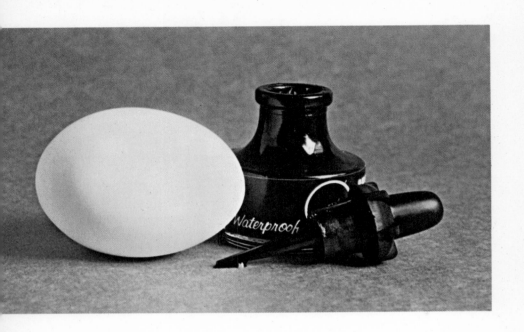

Light is something that makes us able to see when it enters our eyes. Without light everything is dark even if our eyes are open.

Light that bounces off of things is said to be REFLECTED. Light that is not reflected is taken in, or ABSORBED. Things that absorb most of the sun's light look black to us. Things that reflect most of the sun's light look white.

Light comes mainly from the sun. When the sun
sets, its light is gone, and moonlight sometimes
lights the earth. The moon reflects light from the
sun. The stars are other suns that are too far away
to give us much light.

Man has learned how to make light. He makes
it by burning things, or by using electricity. This book
is mostly about the white light that comes from
our sun.

5

Light is one kind of energy. Heat and electricity are other kinds of energy. When something gives off light, that light goes out in straight lines called RAYS. This is called RADIATION. Many rays of light make up a BEAM.

Make a pinhole in the end of an empty carton that is big enough to hold a flash light. Place the box on a table in a dark room. Hold a sheet of thin white paper near the pinhole. A bright circle will show on the sheet. Move the sheet back. See how the circle gets larger but dimmer. Also, see how some of the light goes through the paper. Things that let some light pass through are said to be TRANSLUCENT.

If your darkened room is cold, get a pan of warm water. Place it on a chair below the light beam. The rising vapor may help you see how the light radiates from the pinhole. The light beam is cone-shaped. Its straight edges show that the spreading light rays are traveling in straight lines.

If you place a piece of clear glass between the hole and your eye, you will see that most of the light comes through the glass. Things that let almost all of the light pass through are said to be TRANSPARENT.

If you put a book between the pinhole and your eye, the book will not let the light beam pass through to your eye. Things that won't let light pass through are said to be OPAQUE.

Most things we see are opaque. When sunlight falls upon you, it cannot pass through. Some of it is reflected. Some of it is absorbed as heat. Some goes past the edges of your body and reaches the ground. The ground looks darker where your body will not let sunlight pass through. You call this dark place your shadow.

THE SPEED OF LIGHT

186,282 miles per second in vacuum
186,225 miles per second in air
140,000 miles per second in water
125,000 miles per second in glass

Light travels very fast. Scientists have measured its speed. From earth a light beam can travel to the moon and back in less than three seconds. Light travels fastest when it goes through a vacuum. A vacuum contains nothing at all, not even air. The space between the earth and the moon is a vacuum.

10

Light from a slide projector passes through water in a fish tank.
Notice how the beam changes direction if it enters or leaves
the water at a slant.

When light travels through air, it slows down just
a little bit. When it travels through water or glass,
it slows down much more.

When a light beam passes from air into water or
glass, different things can happen to it. If the beam
enters at a slant, its direction will change. If it enters
at a right angle, like the lines at a corner of a square,
the direction will not be changed. When a light
beam's direction is changed, we say it is REFRACTED.

What appears to be water on the road is really light being reflected from a thin layer of warm air.

Different layers of warm and cold air can change the direction of light also. The air close to the surface of a paved road is usually warmer on sunny days. Have you ever seen a thin layer of sky dancing near the pavement? If so you have seen light reflected by a warmer air layer.

Sometimes there are several layers of still air over a desert. Reflected light from far-off places may be refracted many times between the layers. Distant scenery may be seen hanging in the desert sky. These unusual happenings are called MIRAGES.

12

If light rays enter glass that has a curved surface, the rays will hit each part of the surface at different angles. The many entering rays will be refracted differently. This refraction is very helpful when special pieces of glass called LENSES are used.

If we use a circular piece of glass that is thickest at the middle and thin at the round edge, we have one kind of lens. After a beam of light passes through it, the rays come to a point beyond the lens. This point is called the FOCUS.

Colored beams of light are passed through two different lenses. The beams come together after leaving the lens that is thicker in the middle. The beams spread apart after leaving the lens that is thicker at the edges.

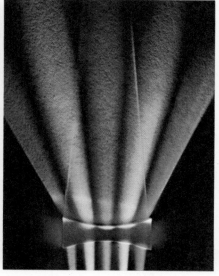

When this kind of lens is used to make tiny things look larger it is called a MAGNIFYING LENS. This is the kind of lens used in a microscope.

If you have a magnifying lens, hold it above a few grains of salt. Move it up and down. Put one eye close to the surface of the lens. Soon you will see the salt particles clearly. They will look much larger; their shapes may surprise you.

These white cubes are really grains of salt as you would see them through this microscope.

 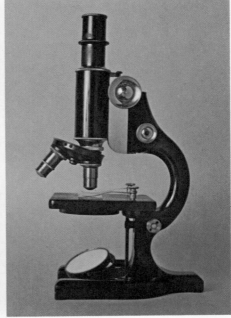

You can make sunlight come to a FOCAL POINT
with a magnifying lens. Move the lens back and forth
over some black paper until you get a tiny bright
spot. As the paper absorbs the concentrated energy it
will begin to smoke and may burst into flame.
Don't look at the spot of bright light very long.

This is the largest reflecting telescope in the world. It was built on Mt. Palomar in California. Can you find the astronomer with a red shirt in the elevator chair?

The magnifying lens in a telescope makes distant things look closer. A REFLECTING TELESCOPE has a saucerlike mirror. The mirror gathers the faint light of stars our eyes cannot see.

16

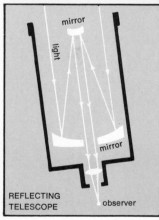

REFLECTING
TELESCOPE   observer

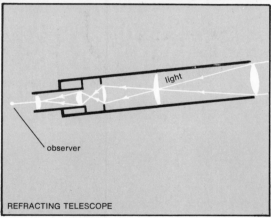

REFRACTING TELESCOPE

The large mirror of a REFLECTING TELESCOPE focuses the light
on a smaller mirror which then focuses the light through an
opening in the main mirror to the observation point.
The boy above is using a REFRACTING TELESCOPE. It contains
a series of lenses that create an enlarged image at the
observation point.

Your eyes contain their own lenses, just inside the dark opening or pupil. The light passing through these lenses is focused on a seeing spot at the back of each eyeball. If the shape of your lenses is not correct, the focal point will not be in the right place. Some things may look blurred or fuzzy.

Far-sighted people have lenses that cannot focus on close things. Near-sighted people have lenses that cannot focus on distant things. Such people are helped by wearing glasses having special lenses. The lenses make the focal point touch the seeing spot again. Then things look clear once more. It is wonderful that man has learned how to use different lenses.

The girl in the background looks fuzzy, just as she would to a near-sighted person. The lenses of the glasses bring her image to a focus so she can be seen clearly.

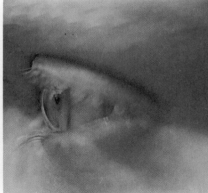

Light energy comes out of atoms in tiny amounts called PHOTONS. Different kinds of atoms give off different kinds of photons; each kind carries a different amount of energy.

Photons of light are said to move up and down rapidly as they speed out in straight directions. Scientists think of them as speeding along with a wavy motion. Photons travel as LIGHT WAVES.

The photons in light cause our eyes to see certain colors. Certain low energy photons make us see the color red. Those with a little more energy make us see orange. With still a little more energy we see yellow . . . then green . . . then blue and finally violet.

This wave model shows how blue, green, and red light waves travel. The blue waves vibrate faster than the red waves, because blue light has more energy than red light. However, all light waves travel at the same speed.

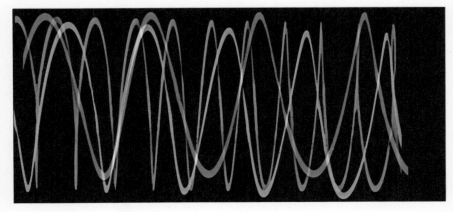

The spectrum on the right is from a light bulb. It contains more red and yellow light but less blue light than the sunlight spectrum on the left.

Sunlight is made up of different kinds of light waves. Each kind has its own length, its own kind of photons and its own amount of energy. The light waves in a sunbeam can be spread out separately. A special piece of glass with three flat sides will do this. Such a piece of glass is called a PRISM.

20

When separated light from a prism falls on a white wall, you can see a band of assorted colors. These are made by the sorted-out light waves. Those having the lowest energy cause you to see the red at one end of the band. Those having the highest energy cause you to see violet at the other end. You can also see other colors in between. A beautiful band is made when you separate the light waves in sunlight. It is called the SOLAR SPECTRUM. Other kinds of light give different spectrum patterns.

A diamond spreads reflected light more widely than a glass prism does. This is why diamonds sparkle so beautifully. They are cut in a special way to act like many prisms.

A rainbow looks like a spectrum, because it is a spectrum. After a rainstorm, the air is still filled with tiny droplets of water. Each droplet acts like a prism. When the sun comes out and shines through the droplets, the photons are sorted out. Then we see a rainbow, a spectrum in the sky.

Sometimes you can see a miniature rainbow in the spray of water made by a fountain.

Some materials absorb all the kinds of photons in sunlight. Then there are no photons left to reflect back to our eyes. Such materials look black to us. Other materials absorb only certain kinds of photons and let the others reflect. These materials look colored to us.

Light-absorbing materials can be added to glass to make it colored. Red glass looks red, because only waves of red light can pass through. All the other photons were absorbed. Blue glass lets only the waves of blue light pass through.

Color does not really belong to something you see.
It belongs to the light reflected from whatever you see.
There is a way you can show how this is true.

24

Any object will appear to change color under colored light, whether it is a ball, an egg or a tomato.

Take a red ball, a green ball and a white ball into a dark room. Shine a red light on them. The red ball will look red and the white ball will look red also. But the green ball will look black.

Then shine a green light on the balls instead. The green ball will look green and the white ball will look green. But the red ball will look black to you now.

It is fun to see what happens when different colored lights are mixed. This can be done using three light projectors with color filters in a dark room. Shine red, blue and green light beams on something close to a white wall. Look at the shadows. You will see white where the three colored beams overlap. Where only two colors overlap you will see a different color. Mixing different colored lights will give you many surprises.

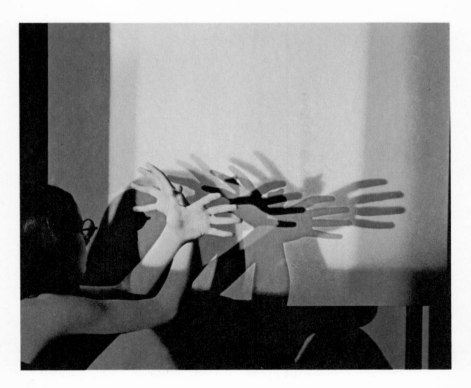

You have probably seen what happens when certain water colors are mixed. If red and green pigments are mixed, a brown results. If red and green lights are overlapped on a white screen, a yellow shows. Mixing colored pigments and mixing colored lights shows us that there is much to learn about color.

Drops of colored dye will mix into beautiful swirls when dropped into clear water. Notice how the blue and yellow dyes are mixing to form green.

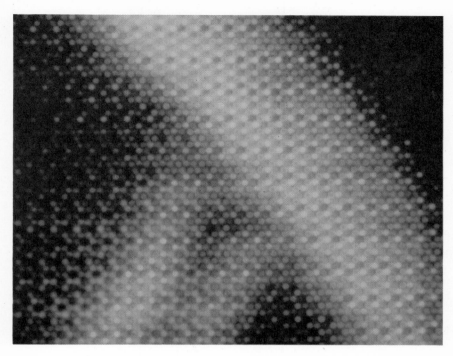

Close-up of the color dots of blue, green and red on a TV picture tube. Where the green and red dots are bright and the blue dots are dark, the picture appears yellow.

Color television uses red, green, and blue light to enable us to see pictures that have all colors. The picture tube is made up of little dots that can produce red, green, or blue lights. These colors are produced in different combinations so that we see not only those colors, but also white, orange, yellow, and violet.

29

For many centuries people have asked, "What is light?" We know that light is the kind of energy that enables us to see.

Words Younger Children May Need Help With

(Numbers refer to page on which the word first appears)

4 reflected
absorbed
6 rays
radiation
beam
translucent
transparent
9 opaque
11 refracted
12 mirages

13 lenses
focus
14 magnifying lens
15 focal point
16 reflecting telescope
17 refracting telescope
19 photons
light waves
20 prism
21 solar spectrum

THINGS TO DO AT HOME OR AT SCHOOL

Make a periscope You will need two empty milk cartons, a scissors, some tape and two small rectangular hand mirrors. You can buy the mirrors in a dime store.

Cut off the tops of the two milk cartons; you will not use them. Tape the open ends of both cartons together. Then cut out two square windows on opposite sides at each end of the long box, as the diagram shows.

Ask someone to help you tape the small hand mirrors inside each window. It is important for each mirror to be taped in at a 45° angle. If they are placed as shown in the drawing you will have made a periscope. You can use it to see around corners or over board fences. It is also handy to use when you are in a crowd and want to see over the heads of other people.

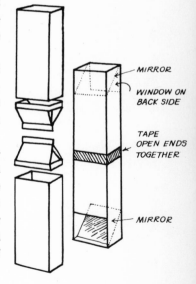

MIRROR

WINDOW ON
BACK SIDE

TAPE
OPEN ENDS
TOGETHER

MIRROR

Make a kaleidoscope   You will need two small mirrors, the same kind used in the periscope above. Lay the two mirrors face to face on the table. Tape them along one of the long edges to make a hinge. Then, stand them up like an open book on a colored picture and look into the mirrors. You will see an image that is repeated. It makes an attractive design. Open the mirrors to different angles and notice how the design varies. See how small objects are multiplied when you place them between the mirrors.

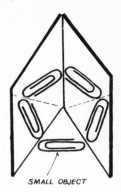

SMALL OBJECT

See how lenses make images   You can have fun using a lens to project images. All you need is a small pocket magnifier or a reading glass. Hold it a few inches away from a wall that is opposite a window. If the light outside the window is bright and the wall is not too darkly colored, you should see an upside-down image of the window as well as what you see outside the window. You may need to move the lens back and forth until you get a sharp image on the wall. The lens in a camera makes images in this way.

Hold the magnifier several inches above the bulb in a table lamp that has a bulb that stands upright. You may have to remove the lamp shade. When you get the magnifier a certain distance above the bulb, the lens will project an enlarged image of the bulb's trademark onto the ceiling. (Most light bulbs have trademarks on the end of the bulb.) This helps you understand how the lens in a slide projector works.